# Benedi Saluto

Sarah Pomie

*Roselle, New Jersey*

Copyright © 2023 by Sarah Pomie

All Rights Reserved.

No part of this book may be used or reproduced by any means, graphic, electronic, or mechanical, including photocopying, recording, taping, or by any information storage retrieval system without the written permission of the publisher except in the case of brief quotations embodied in critical articles and reviews.

This is a work in nonfiction. This book was taken from the author's personal experiences, her memoir captured important segments from her life. Some names and identifying details of people described in this book have been altered to protect their privacy.

For more information contact:
Independent Authors Publications
PO Box 7062,
Roselle, NJ 07203
www.independentauthorspublications.com

Cover Design – Webprint Lab
Edited – Catherine Felegi

Hardback ISBN: 978-1-950974-21-4
Digital ISBN: 978-1-950974-15-3
Library of Congress Control Number: 2023910110

# Dedication

This book is primarily dedicated to God and the Holy Spirit in His glory through His son, Jesus Christ.

Secondly, this book is dedicated to my dear husband, Jean Maxime.

Thirdly, this book is dedicated to my mother, Livie M. Pomie, for all her support. It is also dedicated to my children Keren Kedia and Emmanuel P. Mompoint.

This book is also dedicated to my five sisters and brother, especially to my sister, Roselle Pomie, who has contributed to this project by drawing all the images throughout the stories.

Finally, this book is dedicated to my second cousin, Dr. Gladys Smart, my work supervisor, Carole Simon, Rev. Pastor Gerald, and Deacon Jean Mary Frank, who contributed to my passion for preaching the Word of God.

The only advice I have to all of my readers is - Please take God seriously by accepting Jesus Christ as your personal Savior. Before getting married to someone, take advice solely from God by Jesus and take time to understand and get to know this person very well before you wed.

# Foreword

When I read Mrs. Pomie's book, I had two reactions – one, that once someone has a stroke, the possibility for recovery is minimal. My second reaction was, what can you do after a stroke to stay healthy and remain useful for your community and society?

Having a stroke is frightening. It is a near-death situation - an experience that you don't want to deal with, according to Mrs. Pomie.

I learned a lot about stroke victims - their challenges that could be paralytically damaging. After reading this book, all the preconceived ideas that I had are gone. I now have more considerations for the victims of strokes than I ever had for any type of illness.

Mrs. Pomie was lucky to have her family close to her in a moment that she needed them the most. On the top of everything, she is a Christian - a believer of God. Most people do not come out of one stroke. She survived two. Mrs. Pomie is 95% recovered. She has all her sense, she is capable of driving by herself, and she is in school taking a communications course.

Despite the inconsistent or weak association between cholesterol and stroke, lowering cholesterol concentration with statins reduces the risk of stroke in high-risk populations. Patients with non-cardioembolic can seek other preventive strategies, including individuals with other health issues.

When Mrs. Pomie went to the hospital after the second stroke, the doctors discovered a hole in her heart. The doctors revealed that everything was okay without medication. That was a blessing from God.

To the reader of this book, please be considerate toward stroke victims and those who did not have the chance Mrs. Pomie had.

- Lociano Benjamin

# BENEDI SALUTO

Author of *500 Years of Exploitation, a Study of Diplomacy and Economics in Haiti*

*Tears of Love*, a collection of poems in French and English

*Periple D'Une Vie/A Perilous life/El Viaje de Una Vida*, a novel about my love life story in three languages

Former Adjunct Professor from the Modern Languages Department of Montclair State University

Winner of the bronze medal for a poetry contest by the Institute Academic of Paris in 1998

First prize winner of a poetry contest organized by the French Consulate in New York in March 2000

French teacher at West Orange High School

My experience with God is very similar to Abraham's. In fact, all Christians know the story of Abraham. In the beginning, he was originally called Abram, and his wife's name was Sarai. Right before he was renamed, God said to him, "Abraham, get out of your country, from your father's house, and I will guide you into a new land. I will also make you a great nation. I will bless your great name. Furthermore, I will bless those who blessed you, and you shall then be blessed." At the time, Abraham was seventy-five years old before his migration from Haran into the new land of Canaan.

Thus, Abraham departed as the Lord had spoken to him. He took his wife Sarai and his nephew Lot, along with all their possessions and servants from Haran. In Genesis 12: 7, the Lord appeared to Abraham and said, "To your descendants, I will give you this land." There, Abraham built an altar to the Lord.

In Genesis 12: 11, Abraham's doubt was imminent. Besides, Abraham had personally built a relationship with God while he was demonstrating some fears toward him. My dear readers - God will do everything for you not to be afraid. All you have to do is put your trust and faith in Him.

However, Abraham left his family to serve God without question. God communicated with him all the time, like two people that know each other. When you first meet someone, you don't really know that person. You will learn what they like and don't like. At first, Abraham didn't fully understand the power of God. The main reason God asked him to migrate to Canaan was because the land of Hanan was experiencing an onset of drought and famine, but Abraham trusted God without question.

As they arrived in Egypt, Abraham asked Sarai to lie for him in order to protect him. That's indeed a doubt. God is the biggest protector! <u>The</u> protector! But Abraham didn't know God yet. Know that God forgives you, if you don't know him enough. On the other hand, it's almost the same thing in my personal story sticking out among all, it's me who took it. On the contrary, God has talked to me so many times that I have built a relationship with Him. Now, my faith in God is stronger and correct. I know the existence of God perfectly well. No one can deter me from Him.

My readers, I want to affirm that I now understand the character of God. Even if I was in Haiti, which is currently under socio-political chaos and scrutiny,

I would not be able to leave and migrate to the United States without God's will. I must do everything with the consent of God. Because Abraham went and stayed in Canaan, he survived. After my first stroke, God healed me. Satan is the father of lies, so I decided to preach the word of God. I used to preach every Wednesday at a Baptist church under the leadership of Pastor Metellus.

Since I have made a wish to God by saying, "Father God, I chose to preach your living words all my life." I am so grateful for His fidelity toward my life. Consequently, I devoted my life to His service. So, I began to preach the word of God every weekday in Pastor Metellus's church. One day, I went to the service and spoke with the church leaders and told them of the importance for me to return to work. I forgot that I made a wish to God, but God does not forget. I went to my job and the management wanted me to return to work as soon as possible. They gave me an envelope for the doctor to expedite the process of pre-employment lab work.

The doctor sent me to the lab, and everything was cleared for me to go to work. My job allowed me to work only on Mondays just for observation. During that period of time, I felt a terrible pain that I could not bear. After my terrible day at work, I did not complain to anyone pretending everything was going well for me. The office manager called me and told me that my job status would be full-time. So, on Wednesday, I went to a fasting prayer at the church to testify to my fellow Christians that I will return to work full-time and unfortunately, I will not be able to continue preaching on Wednesdays anymore. They prayed for me, and I went home. I started my full-time status the following morning and everything was very good.

On Saturday morning, I stayed in bed. I was immobilized. My daughter went to work for the day. I wanted to go to the bathroom, but I couldn't move and nobody was home. I stayed in bed until my daughter came home. I told her that I didn't feel good, but she was tired and didn't quite understand my situation. So, I asked her to give me the phone to call my son. My son lives far away.

I explained to him how I felt. My son called my daughter and asked her to take me to the emergency room. When I arrived, it was too late. The doctor told me that, unfortunately, I had another stroke. I was crying like a child when I heard the news.

I had the second stroke on August 21, 2022. I spent one month in a rehab facility.

God definitely tested my faith, as I didn't understand the character of God. Remember, my brethren, when you make a wish to God, He will never forget. My readers, I came home and, after three to four days, I had a vision from God.

I have an older sister who I always thought didn't like me. One day, I had a vision that she was trying to choke me. I almost died. During that moment, I looked up to the sky and saw Ebraique scriptures. In one of them, she insisted to me, "This is the commandment God loves the most. It is important to love your brother as you love yourself." That morning, I woke up and preached about what happened. Again, as we talk about Abraham's life compare to mine, he made a lot of mistakes but God tolerated him. He did not know God's character, but God blessed him regardless. This situation of Abraham and God is exactly the same as mine. This is why I want to dedicate my life to be God's servant and not worry about what tomorrow is going to bring. I have faith in Him and He will always provide for me and my family.

Dear readers, I want you to understand that God created everything for us to live happily. If you read Luck 4: 14-30, these verses state that those preaching the Word of God need to be trustworthy and believe in Him. Jesus is our example. From God's commandment, what He likes the most is, love God with all your heart and love your brother that you see every day. It is despicable to see how one is using the Word of the Lord to convert people, knowing that the brother has not eating for days. It would be very kind to nourish the brother, to help him out with whatever situation his dealing with before you start preaching to him. You have an obligation to feed him if you can afford to do so. Then you will love your brother as much as you love yourself.

The next task you have as a person of faith or as a servant of the Lord is to respect everyone in your circle, religious and non-religious. Don't go to bed angry with anyone. Instead, pray for whomever gets you angry. Apostle Paul blessed the Christians daily with *shalom*. God bless you, Benedi Saluto. Just get on your knees in the morning as soon as you get up from bed, bow your head down, and say the Lord's prayer to start your day with many blessings. Ask Him for mercy and guidance for the day you have ahead of you. Reading the Bible is a spiritual meal. As your body needs food to survive, your soul need prayers.

After my second stroke, I become very spiritual and a good servant of the Lord. Just like Abraham, God was testing my faith in him and I obey his Commandments to this day. God has covered me with His blessings after the two strokes. I consider myself a miracle. No one before me has had two strokes without any sever brain damages or disabilities from the body. You should never doubt God, because He is able. He is a God of compassion.

## BENEDI SALUTO

My fellow readers, no matter what you are going through in this life, always believe in God, because He is the only one that can take you out of that bad situation and spare your life. It is not your family members that are going to save you, regardless of all the good care they can provide for you. God is the answer. Believe me, my brothers and sisters, believe, but you have to keep your promise to God.

Benedi Saluto

# Contents

Chapter 1 .................................................................. 1

Chapter 2 .................................................................. 5

Chapter 3 ................................................................ 35

Chapter 4 ................................................................ 37

Chapter 5 ................................................................ 41

Chapter 6 ................................................................ 43

Chapter 7 ................................................................ 49

# 1.

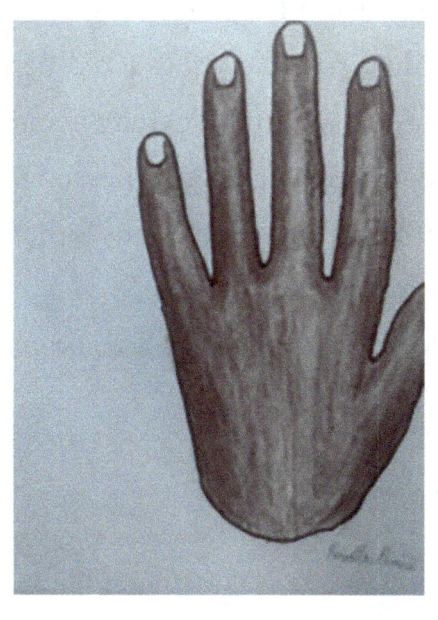

My name is Sarah Pomie. I was born on May 20, 1961 at Grand Riviere Du Nord in Haiti. I was a stillborn. My mother died as well after giving birth to me. My father worked at the hospital, but that day, he was absent. Instead, he was at Radio 4VEH, one of the most listened-to radio stations in Haiti, presenting a show about health. When he heard the news, he asked the listeners to pray and not to bring my mother and me to the funeral home yet.

A miracle was about to happen.

At the hospital, the doctors were Americans. When they noticed non-family members in the room, they asked these new people to identify themselves. My family did, but Madame Charm told the doctors that she was a servant to the family. Whenever there was a party, her job was to serve the guests. But in reality, Madame Charm was a witch, acting undercover to hurt people, especially children. She would operate mostly in the night, doing sorcery. That day, she stood in the hospital room. Madame Charm had on a big hat, so the doctors asked her to leave the room. Once she left, my mom, despite being thought dead, woke up and started singing a gospel song. As she was singing, I started screaming like any other child coming out of labor would have done.

Right after this miracle, everybody applauded. From that moment on, I was alive.

# 2.

When I was thirteen years old, I dreamt that I was in a foreign country, away from my home in Haiti, walking with a folder in my hands. I saw a white man with a saw who told me that if I passed by him, he was going to hurt me. I looked behind me and noticed there was no way for me to go back. My only way out was to go under the saw. I went through, but he was trying to get me. He was very tall, and could have taken one step to cut me into pieces. He was running after me when I reached a house that looked like a church. I ran up the steps to the open door, but before I ran in, I turned to see what was written on the front door. The door said, *Eglise de la Saintete* - The Church of the Saints.

When I entered, I saw three men reading the Bible. They told me to hide behind them. The white man running after me realized that I was being protected by these men, so he stopped and told me that I was lucky. Suddenly, I woke up from the dream.

In order to perfect my French while living in Haiti, I went to the French Institute. Later, I went to Chez Armand Joseph, a business school. I graduated and become a teacher of dactylography at Mr. Eddy Basin's school. In fact, I was the one who started the school for him.

We started with a few typing machines. Within no time, the school became well-known.

I also worked at the Toussaint Louverture Airport under Madame Ertha Pascale Troulliot's administration at the Office of Information, and as a bookkeeper at Mr. Eddy Basin's school in Cap Haitian. Back then, Haiti was the place to be. I had a very good life.

A few years later, my husband, Joseph Berenger, was with me in Cap Haitian and told me that he was going to take me somewhere. He ended up taking me to a beautiful house in Grand Riviere du Nord. There, I saw Madage Charm - the lady who tried to kill my mom and me at birth. Even though she recognized me , she couldn't speak. That was the last time we saw one another, since she died soon after.

When I was 23, I used to sing very well. I would sing at the Second Baptiste Church. The pastor, my mom's cousin, was Rev. Senofar.

There, I met my husband, who was a writer and had recently authored a book on taxation. That day, he was preaching about dues. He was the director of the tobacco company in Haiti, and had the biggest photo studio in Cap Haitian. He was in a good situation and was very polite. During our marriage, we had a son name Georges. Sadly, I lost him to cancer.

I left for the United States to be with my father soon after, who was working as a doctor. He had a few clinics and would give jobs to doctors back in Haiti to work for him. My father would tell me the landlord said only my mother was allowed to come and live with him, but my mom was still working in Haiti. She had not retired yet, so she did not have her pension from Ofatma, where she was a nurse. My little sister lived with him in the apartment as well. He was not expecting me, so it was very difficult. There was not enough space for me to stay there.

I went to live with a friend, but it was still uncomfortable, so I decided to go back to Haiti.

Some family members on my mother's side still lived in Haiti. Even though I didn't know them, they told me they would let me stay for one night. When I told them that I want to go back home, they told me no. I had to find a job first. They took me to an agency. If the agency hired me, I would be able to find a place to stay while I earned a living.

I accepted a job taking care of two boys for $65 per week.

In order for me to go to church on Sundays, on weekends, I would stay at the pastor's house. They gave me a nice room to myself. The pastor's wife was a home health aide companion, so she was not always home. One night, the pastor came to my room, trying to stay there. I was half asleep, but noticed some transformation within the pastor. I don't know if he was trying to turn into a donkey or trying to touch me, but I screamed at the top of my lungs, so he left.

The next morning, the pastor drove the van to pick people up and take them to church. I was there as well. People noticed my voice changed, and understood that something was wrong. They also knew that the pastor's wife worked in New York and was not home.

I prayed to the Lord to please help me get a husband so I could get married and be away from this man.

I had a dream where I saw a short gentleman with two kids. He was going up and down, as though on a see-saw. Soon, I met this man in real life - the same man heard me talking with someone at an employment office, listening to my conversation with the director of the agency. The director knew my first husband and wanted to help me. He put my name down so I could start taking English classes. While I was talking, this man told the director, "The lady that you are talking to has a beautiful voice. Please say hi to her for me." The director placed him on the phone to say hi and we exchange numbers. He started calling me, telling me stories about his wife and child, that his wife worked for a telecommunication company in Haiti, and she was cheating on him with co-workers.

He called me constantly, so one day, I told him, "I have been talking to you for quite some time now, but I don't know what you look like." Since I did not have my green card and I no longer wanted to be single and alone, I wanted to get married. He wanted to meet at a restaurant, but I told him to meet at the director's office - the same place where he spoke to me on the phone. When he saw me, he said that I was beautiful. When I saw him, I called the director and told him that this guy was too ugly. I didn't think it would work out between us. I could not go out with a guy like this. I wouldn't stoop that low.

The director told the man, "The lady says you are too ugly. She is not going out with you." Now, the man hated me with a passion. He was mad.

A few days later, despite how ugly he was, I agreed to go out on a date with him.

He was well educated, and had graduated from college. He did not have a house, but instead lived in a basement. He took me to meet a few of his friends. While I was with him in the basement, I asked him to call his wife in front of me so I could hear their conversation and see if he was being honest. He was not yet divorced so as I was listening, his wife said, "You left me here! You never send money for me to take care of the kids."

It seemed like he was at fault, and I told him that. He then picked up a pair of scissors and tried to kill me right there.

***

I don't like scandals, and that could have been a big one. I had no idea why I accepted his proposal after that, but I needed a green card since I was in the country illegally and did not want to risk deportation, and I did not want word to spread about my situation. I could just marry him, get my paperwork in order, then move on with my life and my children. He took me to a place in Manhattan for the wedding. I called my dad and told him that maybe, this is the husband that God wants for me, even if he is so ugly. My father told me that sometimes, you ask God for something, but the devil moves ahead and gives you something else before you get what God has in store for you; keep on praying.

My new husband took care of all the wedding expenses and even paid for my wedding dress. He invited all his friends. But I suffered from the get-go. When I was having my first child, I suffered. I spoke to people at the hospital and told them I was afraid to go home. I wanted to stay at the hospital.

Two months after the wedding, I became pregnant with my son, Jean. I had to look for a job – something I did not do in my first marriage. When I was with my first husband in Cap Haitian, I my husband provided. I had two servants and two men to watch over the property, as well as take care of the garden.

However, I did my best to cope. He rented an apartment for me and we started living together. Even while pregnant, my husband did me wrong. He did not consider my needs. In the morning, I had to wake up early to prepare him breakfast as he sat at his piano playing music. He treated me like I was his servant. I had to cook, set up the table, clear the table when he was done eating, and do the dishes. While normally, I would do this with pleasure since in my opinion, it is a wife's duty to take care of her husband, it was the way he acted that displeased me. He did not help with house chores at all. On Sundays, as I was cooking before church, he would tell me, "I am getting ready to go to church and I don't have time to wait for you." I would have to drop everything and get ready, but when we arrived, I would be crying. I had no idea why I put myself into this situation. The pastor's wife noticed and asked to talk in private. She said she would talk to my husband after I explained to her what I was going through. Whenever I accompanied him somewhere, he would drive and I would pray. When I was doing prayer in action, praying for the needy, the sick, and for those suffering, he would tell me to be quiet. He was rude and very aggressive. I never lived in this kind of relationship before.

Some days later, the pastor allowed him to preach. I did not know anything about it. My husband's prediction that day was about me. He told the followers that the biggest enemy one could have is a spouse that lives with you and shares the same bed with you. I found out that he chose to preach on that topic because the pastor's wife had spoken to him about our marriage. I became his enemy.

I was still pregnant. One day, I had to go to a hospital in Newark, New Jersey to see my doctor. My husband never cared to look for me, nor to pick me up, so I had to walk from the hospital in Newark to East Orange – a full hour away.

As the nurses were doing the ultrasound, they sent someone to ask me how I was feeling. I replied that I felt depressed. I did not know they were going to take that out of context. I said that sometimes, I wasn't allowed to wash my clothes in the laundry. My husband never gave me the money to buy detergent or to go to the laundromat, so I had to hand-wash everything in the shower using body wash. The person from the hospital called my house. She spoke to my husband and told him what I said. His attitude toward me changed completely.

I went to look for a job with a lawyer who happened to be friends with my first husband. I took the opportunity to explain what I was going through in my new marriage, so he told me to ask my husband to come to his office to help him with his citizenship papers. Through that, I could also proceed with my own paperwork and receive my green card. In no time, my husband became friends with the lawyer and his wife. He spread lies, telling the lawyer's wife that the people from the hospital said I was crazy. Everybody that knew me thought I was crazy because of him.

Just the fact that my husband was saying this affected me. When I went for my second ultrasound, the doctor told me that the baby was in danger. After several tests, they noticed that I had a cyst in my belly that was bigger than the baby. The cyst was a little over two inches. My husband and I met with the doctor, who told us that if I did not receive surgery before the baby got bigger, I was going to die. The cyst was about burst and might transform into cancer. However, if I underwent the surgery, I would have two outcomes - either I would die or survive. I agreed to the surgery. I was four months pregnant when I went through the surgery. If I did the operation before the baby's fourth month, he would have died. They wanted to let the baby grow a bit more to make sure that everything went well. The people from church, my friends, my family - everybody was praying for me.

God wanted to show me that He was the one who did the surgery. While I was in the hospital, I called my family in Haiti to ask them to pray for me but to no avail - every phone was out of service or there were issues.

I kept calling my sister who was a doctor and studied medicine in Bolivia, but no one was available to pick up the phone. I called my little sister in New Jersey, but she was traveling somewhere, and I did not know exactly where. I couldn't reach anyone. God wanted to make sure I knew He was the one doing the surgery. I should not worry.

The night before the surgery, I dreamt about my mother, who came to visit with some bread. The minute I saw my mother, I knew I was safe.

The doctors removed the cyst in my stomach. That was the first time they did this kind of surgery at the hospital. They had medical students there to watch, and videotaped it as well. The surgery was a success. After, they scheduled a follow-up to check on the baby.

A few days later, I was released and went home. My brothers and sisters from the church took good care of me. They cleaned the house for me as well. One night, I was in bed. Nobody was there. I rolled over because I couldn't breathe as I turned over on my belly. I could see the baby moving. It was all white and looked like the belly had turned inside out. My husband felt obligated to call an ambulance, but I could read on his face that he was tired of me. Even though I was in pain, he did not show any sympathy. When the ambulance came, they put me on the stretcher. I felt every single step they took in my stomach. I was in so much pain.

I would not dare compare myself to Jesus, but the suffering that I had at that moment was un-measurable. The suffering continued as the ambulance got on the road to the hospital. When we finally arrived, my situation was grave. The doctors were discussing my case and were very careful not to let me hear what they were talking about. They talked to my husband, and told him that they couldn't give me anesthesia anymore. If they did, it would not be good for me nor my child.

It took them a long time before deciding what to do. They took me to the operation room, where one doctor held my right hand and another doctor my left hand. Two more were at my legs.

They sawed at my belly without anesthesia. The pain was excruciating. I was screaming. After the procedure, the doctors gave me some medication to calm me down. I went back home after the operation. All this to spare my son's and my lives. What hurt the most was when my new husband referred to my first husband and told me how my first husband was someone who always acted superior to others. It seemed like my previous husband did something to my second husband and he was seeking revenge by mistreating me.

While I was going through this trauma, my husband sometimes chose not to buy food for the house, just to make me suffer. I never had issues with my ex-husband like this. He was a wealthy man who cared for his family. The man that I married for my second marriage was a taxi driver. He had a car he bought for the business, and had someone driving it for him when it was not his shift.

One day, I overheard a conversation he was having with one of his drivers. The driver was on his way to the mall to go shopping for his wife and daughter. Since I was starving, I went to see the Coubertin family - one of my husband's friends in the same building where we were living. My husband went to school with him, and was a good friend of the family. I was going to tell his friend that things were not well with me. As someone who was about to give birth, I had no food. However, I had second thoughts. I decided to talk to my other neighbor about the situation instead. She was happy to help me, making pumpkin soup, plantains with meat, and other food every now and then.

The same neighbor who helped me saw my husband one day and told him that I had married a good man in the past. That man was rich and I did not have to beg anyone for anything. She knew my previous husband. My husband found out that I was talking about him with other people and they were aware of what I am going through. He told my neighbor to not listen to anything I said because I was crazy - the people from the hospital called him to tell him so, so they shouldn't pay me any mind.

Even though he had his own taxi business, my husband applied for welfare. The government was paying his rent and he was getting food stamps. He received a check every month. I was in the country illegally so, whenever he received those checks, he used them however he wanted and I couldn't say anything. He had three kids in Haiti who he never took care of, but he filed his taxes and claimed one of his kids as though they lived with him in the United States. He collected over $2,000 in taxes but never gave me a penny. I was living in abject poverty. He had a bunch of food stamps to use every day. He went food shopping every week for $50 for the two of us. I cooked for our family, but he went around and told people that I eat a lot.

He would leave me in the house by myself with the baby and stayed out overnight.

He pretended he was attending medical school, but was actually having the time of his life while I suffered alone with the baby.

One day, I invited my dad over to have dinner. My husband was never home. As I was cooking, my father was seated in the living room. I was preparing chicken. All of a sudden, my husband showed up and did not even say hi to my father. My father left without saying goodbye, since he was so offended. I was very upset. It was so painful. I stayed in the relationship for too long and accepted too much. I reached a point and couldn't take it anymore. I brought my son to the nearest park to spend time with him.

I remember one time, I saw people from where we were living who dealt drugs. My husband was helping them with their bags. I told my husband that these were not the kind of friends we needed. He replied, "Even if I die tomorrow, my corpse will have more value than you." He attended Essex County College in Newark, New Jersey and told everyone that he was studying medicine, but I never left the house. I was his slave. I was babysitting for someone who gave me some change every week. It was a great opportunity to earn a living and have my own money to take care of my baby and myself.

Now that I was doing this part-time job, I was able to send something to my son from my first marriage for Christmas. My husband told me that my son was a bandit, and humiliated my little brother, Herold. He wanted to give a computer to Herold to give to one of his friends in Haiti, since my brother was going there, but when my brother called him to talk about it, he called Herold all kind of names.

During the winter, the house was cold since there was no heat. When I asked him about it, my husband asked, "Why don't you call the police? Then they can tell the people to put the heat on." I did call and asked them if they could call the manager of the building, my cousin, and ask him to put the heat on. When my husband found out, he called my cousin in front of me and pretended that he did not know anything. He never thought I would have done such a thing - call the police on my own family. A few months later, we moved to Maplewood, New Jersey. My husband immediately started telling people in the neighborhood that I was a crazy woman. There was a daycare around the corner from where we were living, so we took the kids there. My husband quickly told them that I was mentally ill.

Later, we had a daughter. When she was born, he did not buy her clothes. I was using my sister's children's clothes from Haiti to dress my own child. One day, he brought a loaf of bread and some bananas, placed them on the top of the refrigerator, and sat there looking at me. He said, "Look, you are a big pig. Don't you dare eat the bread and the bananas that I brought for my kids."

In the midst of all this, I received my green card. Throughout the process, we had a bank account together with $2,000. I was thinking of getting away from this man for good by going back to Haiti and coming back to the United States some other time. I went to the bank, took out $1,000, bought a ticket, and I went to Haiti with my three-year-old daughter. My son was already in Haiti at the time.

My husband went around telling everyone that I stole his baby. I eventually had to return.

At one point, he wanted me to leave the house but not take his children. Life was difficult.

My son was old enough to start school. I wanted to look for a job, so I did everything by myself. I did not have a car to pick my children up from the daycare on time nor a phone, so the daycare would page his beeper to pick up the kids. I arrived late one time to get the children and he was still there. He screamed at me in front of everyone, embarrassing me.

One day, he called the police, telling them I was crazy. According to him, I kept talking nonsense. I was saying to myself how I was living a comfortable life in Haiti and today, I am miserable.

After he had called the police, he told me he was going to kill me - he didn't know how, but he would eventually kill me. I went to the police station to report him for threating my life. They came to my house and kicked him out, telling me that if I wanted to live, I should go to a shelter until I could find another place to stay.

I ended up in a shelter for abused women with my children. They gave us a nice room and fed us well. On Sundays, you couldn't stay on the premises, so we used to go to my sister's house. While living in the shelter, I was authorized by immigration to work while waiting for my green card. Unfortunately, the green card was sent to my former address and my husband received it. He kept it without telling me.

He managed to undo my residence, but the people from the shelter gave me money and helped me re-apply. They also helped me call my husband to court and made him paid child support. He was giving a meager $106 per week for two kids. The daycare alone was $150 a week, which meant the money that he was giving was not enough to even pay for the daycare, let alone food and other necessities.

He abandoned the kids completely, never stopping by to say hi. It was difficult for my son. When we would walk down the streets, my son would look at the taxis to see if he is going to see his father. He did not understand - what was wrong with his dad? Why wouldn't his father come to the house anymore to spend time with him?

Life was tough. I did not know what to do. My husband eventually refused to pay the $106. He thought it was too much for him to give. He would tell me that he was going to take the kids away from me, and that they would be better off with him. Eventually, I agreed, thinking that would allow me to go to school and get a job. Once again, he lied. That was a way for him to stop sending child support. He sent a social worker to my house to investigate me, promising her that he would marry her as soon as he divorced me. My son heard the entire exchange and told me. Sadly, my son became traumatized.

My husband took my furniture and had the nerve to bring other women into the bedroom, having them stay over, sleeping on my bed. He did things he never did for me. He went shopping for the social worker, bought her African dresses, and a brand new white Altima. I was not in the house when he was doing this, but I found out from my son and noticed the difference in my husband. As the mother of his children, I was the one who was supposed to enjoy these privileges, but it was the social worker who benefit from all that instead.

My husband and his new girlfriend would watch pornographic movies in front of my children. I raised my children by teaching them to be the Lord's servant and how to pray to God. To hear that they were being exposed to pornography made me mad. Not only that, he did not feed the kids and was involved with another woman at the same time.

One day, my husband came home to an empty house. The social worker took everything and moved out.

She had her friends from New York come help her move all the furniture. After she left my husband, he came back to me to reconcile. He said for us to get back together for the children, to prepare for their education. I was trapped in his game once again and gave him a third chance. He was worse than the first two times. He told me he came back to me because couldn't find anybody else. Before I even returned to the house, he asked me to take out life insurance. I was crying all the time and he amused himself by calling his friends and making them listen to me over the phone.

He told me repeatedly that within three months, he was going to kill me. He found someone to spend the rest of his life with and wanted to divorce me. My husband took me to New York to see a lawyer to file for divorce. Before the divorce took place, I saw in a dream the wedding ring that he bought me turned black. God undid the marriage. It no longer existed. Even the diamond fell out. I didn't know how did that happened.

My husband wanted to pay $51 in child support, and made arrangements with the lawyer.

When I took my husband to court, the judge asked where did we go for the divorce. I told him that my husband was the one asking me for the divorce and he was the one paying. I did not realize that we were doing something illegal by living in New Jersey while going to New York for the divorce. The judge threatened us both with jail. I called my mother and explained the situation to her. She told me that there was no need to go to New York to have a divorce because New Jersey has competent lawyers. The judge required that my husband's fingerprints and picture taken, and that he be considered a man who abused women. Since I did not speak English very well, they gave me a Creole interpreter. The judge made sure they had my husband on record for his misconduct toward me and the children.

Eventually, I reached a point where I couldn't pay bills. One night, I was praying and in a deep sleep. I dreamt someone entered the room and called my name – Sarah. I smelled something like alcohol and some kind of leaf, and heard someone making a funny noise - "Hooooo!!! Hoooo! Hoooo."

I almost died on May 23, 2001 around 11 PM. The owner of the house was my husband's good friend who was plotting to kill me, but God did not let that happen.

My first son that I had with my second husband died at the age of 21. My situation was growing worse. My husband never showed up to see his kids or called to find out if they were okay. My son was excellent in school. One day, he went to school and was telling people, "You see all these buildings? They are going to disappear because Jesus is coming." During lunchtime, the school administration told me that my son has a problem. They asked me to go see a psychologist with him.

When I went to see the psychologist, the psychologist asked me to stay outside while he talked to my son one-on-one.

My son confessed that he was depressed all of his life, so the psychologist thought he had a mental problem. They took him to the hospital and started giving him medication that had nothing to do with his illness and gave him shots. From that point on, he started having real problems.

I started having problems with him as well. My ex-husband found out what was going on and went to the hospital with a tape recorder as he was talking to one of the doctors. He went, got a lawyer, and sued the hospital. We already sued the hospital when they permanently damaged my son's right arm during his birth, but it takes forever for cases to be solved.

I was the sole caregiver for my son from 2001 on. From time to time, I had a visit from child protective services to check on me, to see how I interacted with the kids.

They wanted to take my children away. I had a friend who lived in Georgia. One day, I asked her to tell me a little bit about Georgia. She told me that it was a little paradise. I asked her to help me find work down there so I could live a better life. Things were not going well for me in New Jersey.

One day, unexpectedly, there was a pastor who came in a van to pick me up and take us to Georgia. When I got there, my life started getting better. I got a job and met Mrs. K at work. She was very good to me, helping me throughout the transition. Mrs. Prince helped me get the job. Mrs. Gerald, whose husband was a pastor, helped as well. I was surrounded by good people.

Whenever I was in a bad situation, the pastor was there for me with the kids. I had a chance to live in a luxury apartment with my children, but my children suffered without their father. Sometimes, my son drew pictures and sent them to New Jersey to him, asking his dad to adopt him. In Georgia, my life changed economically, but the kids suffered from their father's absence.

My daughter started changing her attitude. After school, she started going to the park with her friends. In Georgia, as soon as the sun sets, the kids normally stay home with their families.

Finally, I thought there was a light at the end of the tunnel. The hospital my husband and I sued came up with a settlement and the case was solved. The money was cleared. However, my husband found out and came to look for us in Georgia. I don't know what happened. During that time, my son disappeared. I looked for him everywhere and couldn't find him. The church members were aware, prayed for me, and helped me search.

We found out that my son walked from my house to the highway, trying to get back to New Jersey to be with his father. I don't know if his dad did something for that to happen. The police found him and took him home. The kids told me that they didn't want to stay in Georgia anymore. They wanted to go to New Jersey to live with their dad. I was forced to give away all my furniture and come back to New Jersey with my children.

I rented an apartment in South Orange, New Jersey because I wanted my children to attend good schools.

My son went on to college to become a neurologist. He was brilliant in school, but was still horribly depressed. One day, he went to New York with a flacon of medication and swallowed all of it. He died of an overdose at only 21 years old.

Lots of people came to his funeral. Even some of his elementary teachers came. Everyone was talking about how smart he was. They did not want to open the casket because he committed suicide. They did not let anyone see the body. The police had to spend a lot of time running their investigation. I went through all this misery by myself without my husband's support.

After my divorce, I asked God to give me someone else to spend my life with. This is how God gave me my third husband.

I found comfort after I had a dream. I saw my son as a beautiful baby who opened his eyes and smiled at me. He told me that his passing was wonderful for him. He visited a lot of beautiful places. Ever since, I felt at ease. I don't worry anymore. God gave me a husband who loves me. One day, I told him that if I were doing prayer in action before I met him, I don't think that I would have married him. According to the Bible, if the second husband is alive, I have no right to re-marry anyone else.

God called me when I was thirteen years old but it is only now that I am doing what God wanted me to do.

BENEDI SALUTO….

# 3.

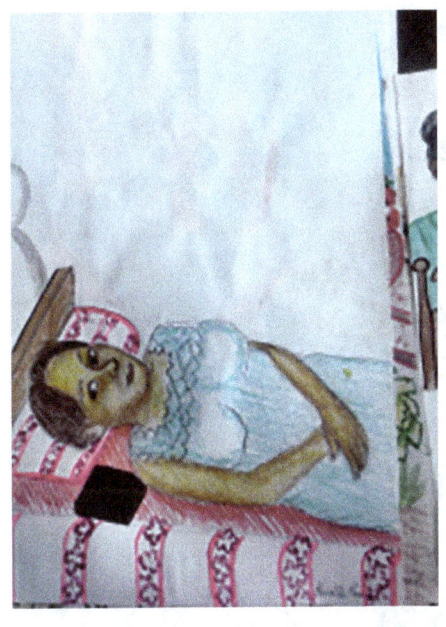

I was fasting in one of my children's room in 2002. I don't remember what month exactly it was, but as I was praying there, I noticed someone who came to the room in a form of a spirit who stood above my bed. It was an angel who did not have eyes, nose, mouth, nor arms. It was just the head and the body. I talked to my pastor, who told me that God had visited me.

# 4.

I remembered a dream in 2004, when I saw the blue sky open with rays of light all around. It was very shiny, like a diamond. I was surrounded by family and there was a plate coming out of the ray of light. People were trying to take it but I was the one who took it. There were a few Black men with long beards on the plate. I did not count how many were there. All of a sudden, I woke up.

    I explained the dream to many pastors and asked them what did they think. They couldn't come up with a good answer. In 2005, I went to Haiti, and spoke to my brother who was living there about the dream. I asked him, what does he think? He told me that the plate represents the world and God gave me a gift.

In my opinion, I thought that God was raising Black people in general and putting them on a pedestal. However, it was not about that - it was about me. God put me on a mission to preach His words to the world, via "Priere en action" - prayer in action.

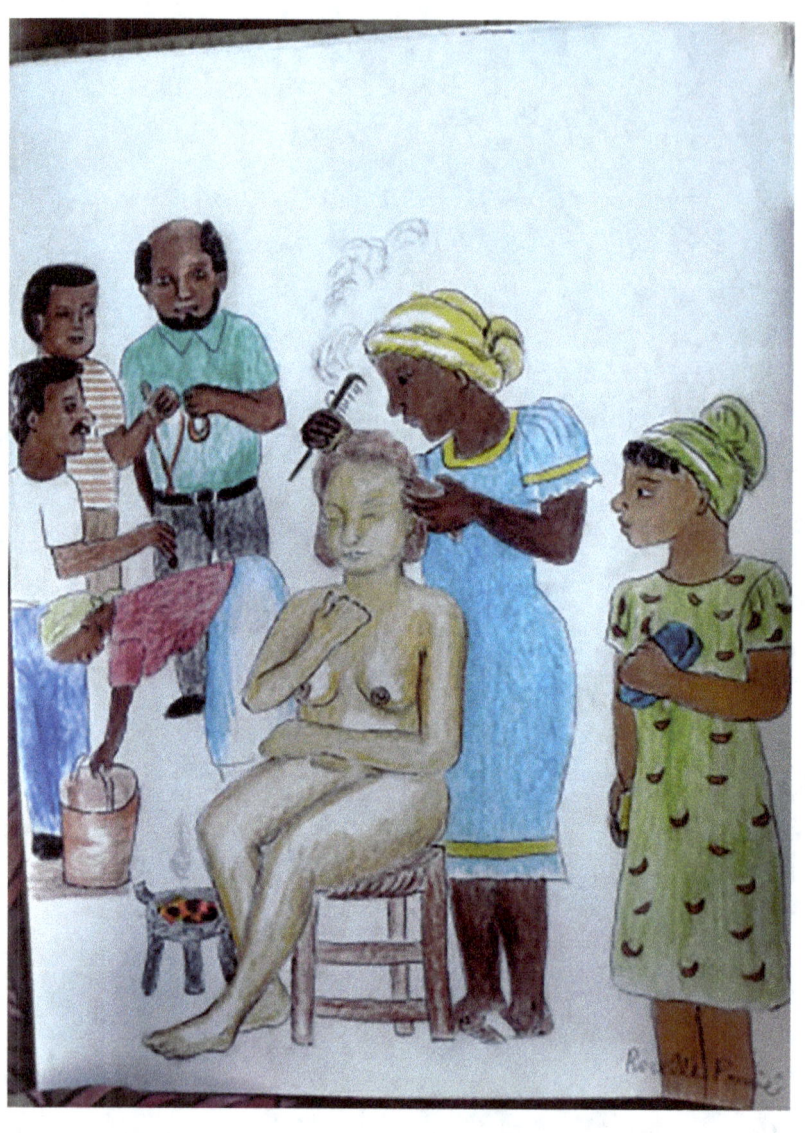

# 5.

In 2011, I was coming from Georgia and travelling to New Jersey, when I had another dream. There, I saw the same Black men who were in the church from my previous dream a long time ago. In the dream, I was thirteen years old. They took off the jewelry that I was wearing and took the jewelry with them. I was asked to sit down by three ladies on a chair, and I was naked. One of the ladies had a very hot iron in her hands. She was taking away the perm in my hair, while the other two bathed me with a sponge and a bucket of water.

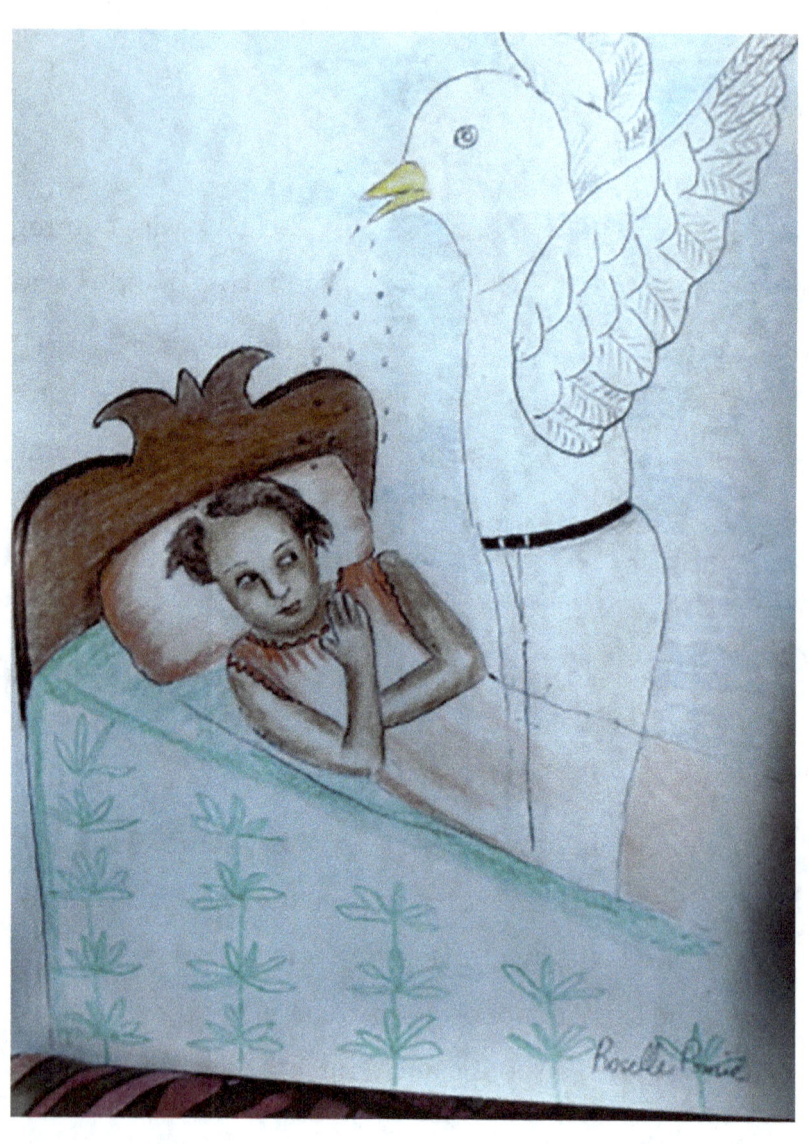

# 6.

I had a cousin, Yvan Smart, who died of cancer in 2022. He was a Seven Day Adventist. At the funeral, everyone was talking positively about him. One of the most important things that I heard was the way he raised his children to fear God.

The same day after the funeral, I went home and wentto bed. Once again, I had a dream. I woke up with prayer in action. Then, I started right away to record my prayers on WhatsApp and shared them to everyone every morning.

While I was doing prayer in action on February 5, 2002, I saw an angel come above my bed and spray tiny snowflakes on me. I was afraid. I left the bed and got on my knees. I was afraid of going back to bed because I thought I was under attack by Satan. I called my cousin, who told me that has nothing to do with Satan, because I was doing a good job. My husband told me that the power of God was very strong with me. That was why I had that thought. Many friends came to me and told me that I had the spirit of God on me. I continued with prayer in action every morning and kept sharing it to all my acquaintances.

On February 10, 2022, I woke up and cleaned my house, cooked, and went outside to my car and took care of something at my bank. It seems like I was guided to take care of those things. While I was getting in my car, there was a neighbor who was usually drunk. He called me and said hi. He had a dream about me but could not tell me about it because I was upset. I told him that I was not upset. Instead, I was very serious.

Everyone in the neighborhood was talking about me, like something was about to happen. My neighbor was about to tell me more about the dream, but I told him that I am a servant of God so He will protect me from any danger. Then I went to the bank and took care of some business because I had a sign that was pushing me to do these things.

I came home and sat on my bed. I noticed the house was turning upside down with me. I felt like vomiting, but that did not happen. I felt so bad that day, I ended up calling my son who lived a few towns over. My son called my daughter who came as quickly as she could, and did a check-up on me. She told me that everything was normal. I told her that I was not feeling well, and asked her to call 911. When the ambulance arrived, the paramedic who came asked me to stand up, but I couldn't stand up on my own.

Prior to that, I used to dream that I was going to die. They were going to take me to the cemetery and cover me with death. As I was walking, there was always a cliff to my right. The angel who had visited me had a man face and a bird face from time to time. As he stood above me, he spread something on me, like some kind of powder, but they were like snowflakes.

The day the paramedics took me to the hospital, I was having a stroke. I couldn't feel anything on my right side.

That was the reason why I was seeing the cliff on my right as I was walking in my dream.

I was damaged on my right side, my mouth and face were twisted, I was paralyzed and I couldn't do anything for myself. I was like a baby. Water would run out of my mouth. I couldn't speak. I was mumbling.

After seven days in the hospital, the doctors decided to send me to a nursing home for therapy. I couldn't walk. After two weeks, while I was in bed, I was doing prayer in action. I felt something like a bug on my side. I turned around to see if there was an insect walking on me. I went from the bed to the chair. After that, I started walking. They sent me to a different room for therapy. I was able to walk on my own to go to therapy with my walker since that day.

On March 24, 2022, the doctor came and told me that I was good enough to go home. He would sign me out. I spoke to my husband and told him the good news. The next morning, a Friday, the nurse in charge came and told me I was leaving. I responded I was willing to go home, just ask my insurance to give me some kind of transportation.

I said to God, "If you want me to serve You with my one solid side, I will serve You with no problem." God heard my prayers and He was helping me. Even though I was in the hospital bed, I was still doing prayer in action. I was singing in a different tone of voice.

God healed me very quickly. It was a miracle. I went home and everybody was surprised to see me. I came home on Friday 25, 2022, without a cane, walker or wheelchair. I took the stairs, opened my door and went inside. On Saturday morning while I was in bed, a man came and said in my right ear, "Benedi Saluto!". I called some pastors, they said to me that they have never heard this word in their lives.

# 7.

Because God spoke to me and said, "Benedi Saluto," you should place your faith in God, because those who have faith in the Lord shall be saved. God said in John Chapter 14, verse 14, "Whoever calls the name of the Father, He shall answer them," and in John Chapter 14, verse 12, "God said the spirit shall bless you."

There was a little boy who had a fish and some bread in his hands. When Jesus called him and said to him, "Give me the fish and the bread that you have in your hands," Jesus took the fish and the bread from the boy and he multiplied them, feeding everybody that was there.

I have seven stages of perfections given to me by God.

I was born on May 20, 1961. I am the second child of my mom. Before she was even pregnant, she said that she was going to call me Sarah. This was a coincidence, because when my mom gave birth to me, the nurse's name was also Sarah. Everything that happened in my life happened miraculously.

Everything that happened in my life proved to me that God exists. I can preach very well without attending theological school. My story is like Joseph's story - Joseph was different from his brothers. They abused him and sold him as a slave. He went to Potiphar's house as a slave but he became the chief of the house. His brothers lied about him and put him in jail, but he became a chief while there. He fed the world.

God chose me to be his servant. Everything I say here in this testimony is the truth. You just need to have faith. If you ask to see God, He will let you see Him. Jesus has said that no one has seen God. God used to communicate with Adam and Eve but after they sinned, God called on them but they did not answer. They went into hiding because they were sinners.

God has spoken to Moses on Mount Sinai and he told Moses, no one has ever seen the Father. Therefore, the Father is Jesus. He sent Moses to Israel to deliver the people from slavery. He gave him the Ten Commandment to share with the people of Israel. He went and talk to the people. His voice was so loud, there was thunder. If someone say that Jesus is not God, that is not true - Jesus is God.

At the beginning was the Word and the Word was with thee, and the Word was God. Who is the Word? The Word was Thee. Jesus called for the sun and sun came. He called for the moon and the moon came. That shows you that Jesus is the Word.

The Word was transformed into human and the human was Jesus. Jesus was among us. Jesus was God living among us. Benedi Saluto. That is what God told me on Saturday, March 26.

Then on Sunday, March 27, I went to church and gave my testimony to my fellow worshipers.

I would like to thank God for all He has accomplished in my life. He is the one in charge of this book. I thank Him for inspiring me with the title of this book, BENEDI SALUTO.

I would like to thank my mother who God allowed to carry me for nine months.

I would like to thank my other half, the person that is in my life right now, my husband. When I had the opportunity to tell him about my suffering from my previous relationships, he counseled me and helped me carry on throughout my trouble time.

I would like to thank the family of Yvan Smart, who unfortunately has passed. I went to his funeral and everyone spoke very highly about him. He was a language professor, a math professor, and he was someone who knew the Bible very well. A big thank you to his sister, Dr. Gladys Smart. I am very grateful for what they have done for me.

A big thank you to my brother, Jean Frank, who led me to be a preacher, and introduced me to a congregation to preach at. He is a leader at Pastor Metellus's church.

It was a Wednesday morning. When I preached at the church, I was so happy, I ended up crying. I would like to thank everyone who, one way or another, encouraged me to write this book, such as my children. I would like to thank Mrs. Roselle Pomie, my sister. She is the one who drew for this book. She is a wonderful artist, and could be looking at you and draw your portrait on the spot beautifully. She is a gifted child. She also designs clothes. She is an excellent cook.

My thanks go to Mrs. Emile as well. She goes to Pastor Metellus's church.

I want to offer my appreciation for Sister Gerald, Pastor Gerald from Georgia, as well as my appreciation for Sister Carole Simon from Georgia.

My thanks go to Pastor Frantz Phillippe. He is the one who introduced me on the radio. He used to play on the radio every morning my prayers in action for his audience.

May God bless everyone that is going to buy this book. God has shown me the way despite all the difficulties that I have encountered in my life, but I have seen the light at the end of the tunnel.

BENEDI SALUTO…

www.ingramcontent.com/pod-product-compliance
Lightning Source LLC
Chambersburg PA
CBHW062141280426
**43673CB00072B/90**